From the frontispiece of Hildegard von Bingen's Scivias

HYMNAL FOR CATASTROPHE

René Bennett

An Imprint of Mouthfeel Press

ACKNOWLEDGEMENTS

"Notes from Palace Walls" first appeared online in *LIGEIA Magazine.*
"Marx and Madonna have a chat at Death & Co." was first printed in *The Gallatin Review.*

The sheet music for "Willing & Able" is public domain and was borrowed from free-scores.com.

The image from St. Hildegard is in public domain: Wikimedia Commons: https://en.wikipedia.org/wiki/File:Hildegard_von_Bingen.jpg

Hymnal for Catastrophe

Mouthfeel Press is an indie press publishing works in English and Spanish by new and established poets. We publish poetry, fiction, and non-fiction. Our print books are available through independent bookstores and online booksellers, or at author's readings. CLASH! Chapbook Series is an imprint of Mouthfeel Press.

Cover Art and Design by Cloud Cardona

Contact Information:
Mouthfeelbooks.com
Info.mouthfeelbooks@gmail.com

ISBN: 978-1-957840-38-3

Published in the United States, 2024
First Printing in English
$12

Contents

for Bowie and D., my shooting stars

Hymnal for Catastrophe

Prelude (On Body/Mind)

The asteroid swims towards Earth
at a rapidly increasing velocity
though we don't know it yet—

how can the mind process what the body
has not experienced?
Or,
how can we think without the material
with which to shape our thoughts into ripe
fruits of understanding?

The first time I twisted my brother's
wrist in rage until red marks
eradicated the boundary between us
is when I learned not to trust the idea of
mind, which knows only itself.
The body senses the presence of a world filled
with what loves us, what will destroy us—
it becomes in fact a form of mind
(when it comes to reality,
that state of absolute multitude).
Without the body we are a solar system
consisting of only a starving sun,
doomed to loneliness,
and perhaps separating it (the body)
from mind (which knows only itself)
was just a means of justifying
violence (the impulse reaction to believing only in yourself).

But how much longer can we sequester the body
when even the telescope appears like an eye
longing for the presence of another?

Hymn for the Harvest

Sometimes when you look up at the bloom of a night sky it almost appears to be trembling on stilts, and you want, for a moment, to see it collapse, instantly crushing our limbs into shards of an obsolete civilization. In a seamless vision you see all of humanity swept up in a ballet of fire: great destruction, the weight off your shoulders. The foremost motive for making God was to ensure that he will destroy us. Scripture reeks of obliteration. Catastrophe ignites the quill, churns our muscles: Revelations gush across the page—maybe a literal take on Montaigne *(that to philosophize is to learn how to die)*.[1]

But I am less interested in Montaigne than in David Bowie, Ziggy Stardust. Bowie who imagines the end of the world, not in a fabulated attempt at eschatology, but in what comes before, five years before, to be exact.[2] In the prefatory panic, individuals emerge as incredible clusters of matter, collectively a material anomaly amid that universal quality of indifference; they are "nobody people," they are "somebody." At the sight of people oblivious in the theater of the everyday, Bowie laments—laments for the impending doom of the people, yet also for the devastating fact of needing them.[3] Because even a lament depends upon one who can hear, who can understand it, whose language is the breath of your own language, just as my words are blowing their imprint along your synapses. This is to say that we must confess out loud how we need one another, how jointly we form a pulsing, perambulating beat of life, susceptible to suddenly being smeared out of sight. We are as vulnerable as a loose tooth, yet only now, under the glaring halo of an approaching asteroid, do we seek out each other's faces in desperation.

Death is not enough; we must anticipate the complete extinction of the species. We must set flames to space and time. And in the penumbra of this grandiose catastrophe, we might see ourselves for what we are. Hence, a necessary revision of Montaigne: that to live is to learn how to become extinct.

I resurrect others who once saw in our lavish fate a chance at redemption. Namely, medieval mystics, fatalistic renegades, peasant revolutionaries:

2

Joachim of Flora, Jean de Roquetaillade, Hildegard von Bingen, Thomas Müntzer—forebears of Bowie, my visionaries, my angels of death—your wings beat the air heavily against my papers, sending them aflutter.

Joachim is clad in monastic rags, tracing history into the earthen floor. He splits time into three sweeping stages; between each occurs an apocalypse to precede the dawn of a new paradigm. Hildegard is playing her psaltery and constructing a language while having visions of "a burning light, as large and as high as a mountain, divided at its summit as if into many tongues."[4] And from this light steps Roquetaillade, carrying an alchemist's clay vessel—

Roquetaillade who sang the echo of David Bowie, that "for five continuous years there will be horrendous novelties in the world."[5] During these five years there would be a reversal of the roles of predator and prey, in direct tandem with the reversal of the peasantry and nobility, a violent overtaking of the predatory upper classes: "the people will rise up and devour the traitorous noble tyrants in the mouth of twice-sharpened swords."[6] Finally, shepherding the revolution, having been tortured endlessly for his fervor, Müntzer's dismembered head, skewered onto a golden staff, calls out, "Oho! How ripe are the rotten apples! Oho! How ripe are the elect! The time of the harvest is here!"[7]

Oh Müntzer, nobles, and savages, how else could we see eye to eye except if staring together into the fire of our annihilation? I don't need to dwell on the phonetic similarity between *revolutions* and *Revelations*. Müntzer was certain in his conviction that the peasant revolution against feudal tyrants would coincide with the end of the world, for only with their lives on the brink might the tyrants be shaken from their pride. Only then could we reap our humanity.

And now we weep that the harvest had not come sooner, for Müntzer who sowed the pastures of insurrection was prematurely put to death, and the nobility has been unable to mark the overpass from the death of the individual to the extinction of the species. This is a fatal fallacy. The conviction that the laborer's singular wasted life is merely another expendable entity, dispelled back into the exhausted repetitions of production and consumption, fails to account for—or denies—how each person is inextricably woven into the survival of the feeble species, holding it up with overworked arms.

Oh nobility, oh chief executives and policemen and children of wealth, who are isolated from Bowie's insistence on other people, we are all tied up in nature's thorns, and those least equipped to admit this defenselessness will be the first to spoil and wither away in their guarded loneliness.

Oh catastrophe, we gravitate towards you. We are teetering between meaning and oblivion. We close our eyes for the asteroid winks in the distant night. The prophecy is true. Eternity meets the slaughterhouse. Collectively we die.

Or maybe more to the point: collectively we live. What happens when we meet each other's panicked eyes under the smoldering sky? When we hear our own heartbeats pounding through our ears, David Bowie playing on full volume? The news anchors will cry on live TV as air raids blow up the enemy's bunkers. Food will become as scarce as tranquility, looted from shelves and devoured by fires. Maybe we'll fight tooth and nail over scraps of vegetables and broken cans, flashing knives at whomever comes too near us. Or, maybe we'll end up letting ourselves starve. Maybe we'll love each other.

The harvest is coming.

How the Body Is Like a Price System: Prayers

1.
The harvest is coming.
I am picking my teeth with a razor blade.
I am reading a manual with colorless photographs
entertaining skewering my eyeball with my locker key.
I am off to a good start.
I put my soul in an airtight jar.
I run my fingers down the staircase railing.
I run my head under water, always running
to catch the next full moon.
I can't feel my limbs.

2.
I am standing in line.
I am gliding along the railroad tracks
wavering off the tracks collapsing
under summer heat.
I am beating someone's meat in the back stockroom
foregoing shipping standards.
I am shutting a screaming baby into a corrugated box
and putting it on tomorrow's to-do list.
I am gnawing on my fist
so I don't tell another lie.

3.
I am standing in line so close
to the person in front I could lick
their nape I could collapse into the arms of the one behind me.
I am having a cursing competition with children
for minimum wage.
I am scanning a box and
I am sliding the box into a plastic bag and
putting its loops over the scowling woman's fingers
which will put it into another plastic bag
which will get dumped into this planet's penniless pastures

and survive there longer than the lifespan of the human species.
I write my boss a note, evoking cancer.
I watch my shadow, from the sidewalk, get hit by cars
and not feel a thing.

4.
I am standing barely
collecting tip jar coins in my teeth so when I smile
cents rain out of my mouth which has become
desensitized to the trick of light,
the glimmer, twinkle slit of white,
my good-days and sleep-tights
and try-not-to-die-on-the-clocks.
I am off to a good start
when I slide a match across red phosphorus
and ignite the night shift to keep warm.
I am crumbling to ashes inside.
I think I'm moving up.

Notes from Palace Walls

Last night I crashed Daddy's Tesla and the evening sky exploded into moonlight and in the wreckage and in the radiance I saw rays of an archangelic clarity, the face of Gabriel, soft and sovereign, holding golden lilies, saying I must reevaluate my definition of success.

I've been seeing the Madonna every night in my dreams lately, or at least some belladonna of false hope. Her holy hands clench around my wicked throat and I suffer to be revived in her hold. Oh god, I want to be revived, I need a life supply of lullabies, not these silvery threads popping pills nor the fear facing my sterilized sunset-colored impression of reality. It's all pretend, my friends are paper cutouts, falling flat at the slightest breath.

I am reevaluating my definition of success.

I pull hymns from my head that haven't been remixed yet, they venerate the rundown cabaret, shameless heartache, naked bodies thrown into space. Behind my puerile American dream it's all parting and departing, construction destruction reconstruction redestruction flames on the mattress, on the walls.

Get me off this acropolis. In my alcoholic dreams of Her I unleash it: I am overloaded, undernourished, treading undercurrents of an unremembered lifetime. When we're dancing mechanically on the rooftop I always ponder jumping off, setting my status to ground zero, where no one can watch me. We're holding hands, they're all colorless and cold, going to no Heaven, overdosing in cities of gold. I float along these strobe-lit roads that go nowhere and I can't stand it. I can't stand the palace. I can't stand the drive.

But when we crashed I felt alive, I was trembling all over heartbeats in my eyes and in the sky. Insobriety. The taste of blood. Angelic devastation. There is no vision of prosperity, which is so uneventful anyway, a term that manufactures success on cyber riches and swimming pools filtered by dissociation. No it was a vision of sincerity and the Angel was promising me things more beautiful than chandelier lights and as they pulled my limbs from the crushed and battered automobile he showered me with lilies and as I gazed skyward from the stretcher he kissed between my eyes, he set me alight, something shivered in the blue night and I saw clearly a shimmering absence: they call it paradise.

Survey

1. Please state your date of birth.

2. Please state your current residence.

3. What is the highest degree or level of school you have completed?

4. What is your current employment status?

5. What is your current emotional status?

6. Please rate how emotionally satisfied you are from 1-5.

7. How many times do you have sex, on average, per month?

8. Do you fuck with the lights off?

9. If so, does your body become the dark or does the dark become your body?

10. If a ball of wax is brought near a fireplace and melts, how do you know it is still wax?

11. Do you believe that a human being is a rational creature?

12. Or have you ever caught your reflection in the windows of a speeding train that you just missed, fixed but gripped in perpetual motion like a riptide, and felt the chokehold of this perceived immutability seize you in your step, until the last train car escapes into the underbelly of some city and your reflection disseminates into something forgotten?

13. How often do you find yourself unable to retain a grasp on what it is that makes you yourself? Rate 1-5.

14. Is a ball of wax still wax when it melts?

15. Suppose you walk upon a rotting corpse in a forest—and this time you didn't miss the train, so you are not in low-spirits when you walk upon this corpse, jaundiced and gnawed-on. Do you flee or do you look into its liquescent eyes and remember the first time you were so enamored with someone that it kept you up all night?

16. Suppose you look into its liquescent eyes and wonder if this is that person.

17. Suppose it is.

18. Or is the rotting corpse made of wax?

19. Refer to question 6 and specify any changes to your response.

20. If this survey weren't anonymous and everyone you know enough not to stumble on their name read your responses, would you be proud of yourself?

21. Or would your tongue swell up, your eyes seek out something certain, something with a name, something steady, something rational to excuse yourself?

22. Do you fuck with the lights dim so you can melt like wax into the half-visible haze?

23. Do you fuck with the lights dim so you can pretend you don't exist?

24. Do you often pretend you don't exist?

25. That you are both solid and liquid at once, and maybe because of this, neither, that the human body is not a fixed thing, but a blur in a window, a flailing fireplace (this isn't pretending), a nose-bleed, a weeping mother, a rotting corpse?

26. Remember? You ran from the corpse?

27. How could you be so careless? Rate 1-5.

28. Is a fire still a fire if you've never felt it burn you?

29. Have you brushed your teeth today?

30. Have you tried to forgive yourself?

31. Try to forgive yourself.

32. Try to forgive yourself.

33. Try to forgive yourself.

Marx and Madonna Have a Chat at Death & Co.

When I say that history is materialistic
I mean that a Gucci sweatshirt
is a symbol of political power.

The person with the biggest house
probably makes the biggest decisions
about the provisions of every other house.

Who owns air conditioning? Who owns electricity?
Who owns the light that illuminates
our bodies trying to make sense of one another
on a box-spring bed?

We depend on these cutouts of matter:
the last scraps of clear water
the shape of a dance floor that guides our feet,
the glasses in our hands, molding our fingers
into place as we drink to our defenselessness. All we know
is this material fabrication,

the bartender, the men in their balmorals,
the woman asking for change at the door,
all steered into place
by the chief suppliers of history.

When I say that history is materialistic
I mean that we are spinning
towards an end in which even our exhaled breaths
have become consumable, I mean that

the fate of our collective body is material
and I'm an immaterial girl.

Willing & Able

*to be read aloud over the melody of Bach's "Jesu, Joy of Man's Desire"

"I try to keep my head up and look the world in the face.

—Edith Maxwell[8]

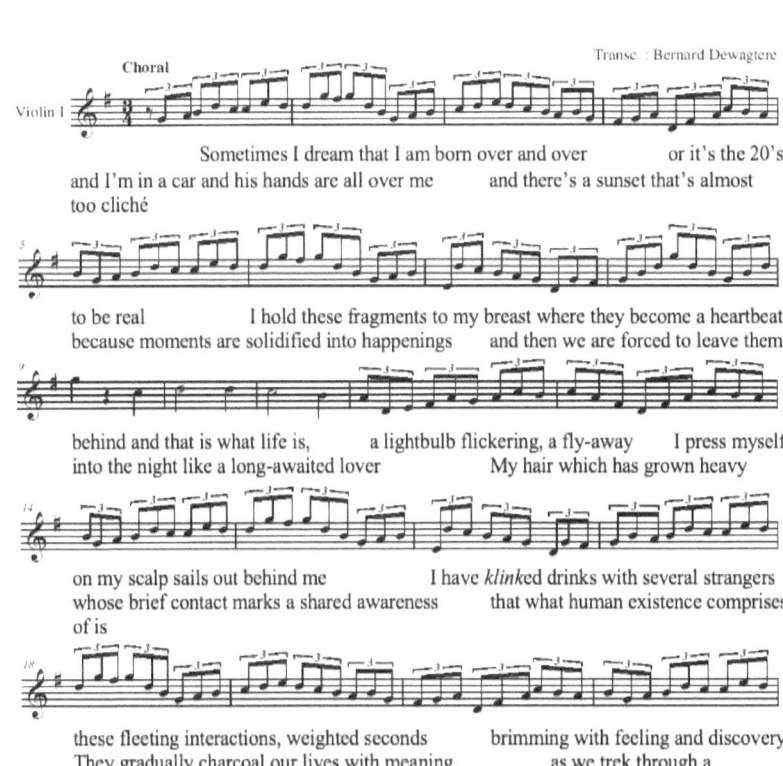

Sometimes I dream that I am born over and over   or it's the 20's
and I'm in a car and his hands are all over me   and there's a sunset that's almost
too cliché

to be real   I hold these fragments to my breast where they become a heartbeat
because moments are solidified into happenings   and then we are forced to leave them

behind and that is what life is,   a lightbulb flickering, a fly-away   I press myself
into the night like a long-awaited lover   My hair which has grown heavy

on my scalp sails out behind me   I have *klink*ed drinks with several strangers
whose brief contact marks a shared awareness   that what human existence comprises
of is

these fleeting interactions, weighted seconds   brimming with feeling and discovery
They gradually charcoal our lives with meaning   as we trek through a
thoughtless cosmos

I make beer-breathed love to the bartender before he drives me back home   under
stars that transfigure into the shapes of goddesses   It is here that I see the
boundlessness

of our doings, for a single action may alter every constellation   And from my house
in the impassive Appalachia

there comes   a low humming like the sound of two people becoming lovers
It is drawing me towards an unseen edge   on which stands my father

waiting in overalls and rage   He tells me I am no person, just an object of his
tether   His speech burns the tobacco stuck between his teeth

slowly churning smoke towards our rooftop   I see smoke gathering, undulating
above as his palm   crashes against my face, and in the smoke

I see shapes take on specific meanings, the harvest of our actions: we move into
each other, away from each other

around the sleeping lioness,   over the embers of permanent flames, further and
further   down the vaulted passage that echoes our inglorious breaths

I am bared to this earth and I'm   willing and able, wavering and capable
I grab that object that has picked battles with gravity

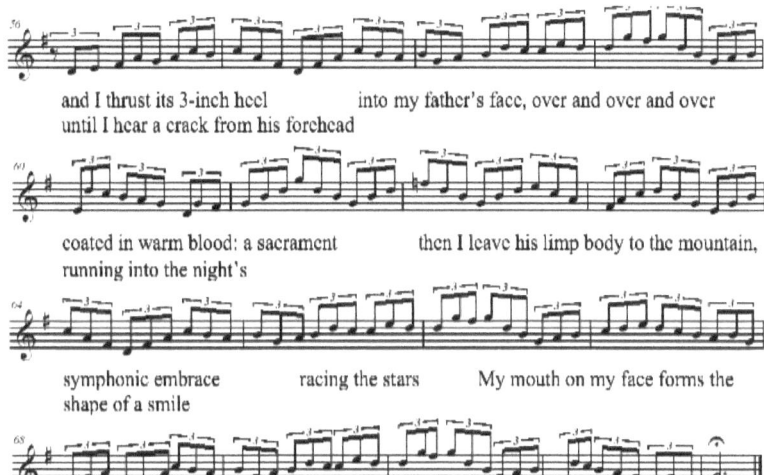

and I thrust its 3-inch heel   into my father's face, over and over and over
until I hear a crack from his forehead

coated in warm blood: a sacrament   then I leave his limp body to the mountain,
running into the night's

symphonic embrace   racing the stars   My mouth on my face forms the
shape of a smile

The Ecstasy of Saint Hildegard[9]

What shapes spirit?
I ask you this as a way of asking myself, for this is the question underlying the visions of Saint Hildegard, Sybil of the Rhine, Prioress of Dreams. What stirs our beliefs, what moves us towards action, how do we respond to being born?

Vision Four:
Hildegard picks up her ten-stringed psaltery in the evening glow that flows from the modest window of her monastery. The strings' vibrations run from her fingers through her arms and breast to her skull, where they perch upon solitude, unlock a consciousness. *A person is recognized by his face, sees with his eyes, hears with his ears, opens his mouth to speak, feels with his hands, walks with his feet; and so the senses are to a person as precious as stones and as a rich treasure sealed in a vase.* Even for one so committed to the soul, the senses burst through her visions. They structure us; they foxtrot in our hearts; they give every hiss and every fuck the tangibility of a thing pumping through us as a lifeblood. Hildegard strums a final, dissonant chord that echoes through the vaults of the monastery.

Vision Three:
I am only trying to make sense of everything (of music, of words, of the transience of these things). Maybe this is what underlies my visions of St. Hildegard's visions of the Universe. *Invisible and eternal things are made known through visible and temporal things.* On a tablet she spells out her longings in a language entirely new, as if the only way to make sense of our thoughts is to invent a language just for them. *Human beings, struck by the grandeur of this miracle, tremble in body and soul, pondering, in their wonder at this miracle, their own weakness and frailty.* She cups her hands in a basin of water and pours it onto her forehead, letting it run down her eyes and lips. I have a headache as demanding as a prophecy.

Vision Seven:
I superimpose all of my lovers into a single image: the face of God. Is this the God of Hildegard's visions? Is this the spirit that burns through her eyes? *I saw a burning light, as large and as high as a mountain, divided*

at its summit as if into many tongues. It is this image that strikes me the most, the frontispiece of her Scivias: red tongues of flame-like substance pouring into Hildegard's eyes as she writes. *The left hand of the destroyer signifies death.* St. Hildegard is dead. My ex-boyfriend is in the hospital. Rent is due next week. *The mental capacity of mortal humans is insufficient to understand the manifold variations of its poisonous fury and malicious exertions.* St. Hildegard is on her knees, trying to make sense of these sights, her head thrown upwards, terrified and ecstatic. She sees an end; she sees everything coming together and apart; this is all that's left: a vision of total destruction.

Litany

Let the house
burn, let the tattered sofa and stained chairs
burn, let the framed outlines of us in the sand
burn, let the roof collapse and the shingles
burn, let it spread from yard to yard until the suburbs all
burn, let the church and the bank and police stations
burn, let the planes catch a tongue of flame and
burn, let piles of fur coats with their possessors
burn, let sidewalks and beggars
burn, let starving children and Swiss vaults
burn, let Montecito villas and nepotistic militias and Creek Blaze
burn, let the Capitol in its incendiary white
burn, let drone warfare and rainforests razed by industrial commercialism
burn, let Wall Street and Hollywood
burn, let the weddings
burn, let the skylines
burn, let every city, let every citizen
burn, let them all
go up in flames, let us
start over again.

Hymn for the Holocene

When you awaken in the middle of the night you find yourself dumped into life like an oil spill. What appears as a shooting star crossing overhead in speechless blaze is actually a premonition of global catastrophe. It strikes you in these moments of strange disenchantment, in the middle of the night, or in a shower with no heated water, or when you're fucking a stranger and it all seems kind of blurry: what if, what if, what if. The sound of an ending, or of an era thrumming all around you. There are no stars visible tonight; in their void is this drifting spirit, not quite visible but perceptible all around, crooning its tempers and misgivings. The spirit of order and crisis, of wildfires and hurricanes, the spirit of David Bowie dying, the spirit of crying through mascara, or pretending to on camera, the spirit of summers getting longer, of executives getting richer, the spirit of words becoming tired, of pandemic, of distance, of fear of one another, the Holocene rupturing, we are now in the third millennium, amen.

This is perhaps what Raymond Williams referred to as a "structure of feeling," what gives an era its breath of life: the Holy Spirit, spirit of our times, *zeitgeist*, the preconscious paradigm, it is what lingers in our fingertips at the end of each day, it is the *this, here, now* sensation that rests upon everyone at once.[10] We shape and are shaped by these structures of feeling every living moment—though I channel the sympathy of a mystic in warning that "feeling" may mislead us to believe this is spontaneous and confined to the individual, when really spirit emerges from collectives, stirred by the slightest agitation.

But we talk of the world as if it is a static thing. There is motion everywhere, every awakening is a motion into living, every word moves along soundwaves and leaps from body to body. When we speak of all periods we are speaking of one grand Holocene, rippling with movement—a plane of infinite variation. We ask ourselves therefore, what moves us? Who dictates spirit? (Trying in vain not to be sucked back by time like some lost memory of you.)

Bowie, on his space-age ballad "Starman," sings of a messianic being who sends a message of hesitant hope to Earth from afar.[11] The starman is only ever waiting, only ever suspended in the sky, while the people below reckon with their imminent apocalypse. I have always considered this song to be tinged with a sad longing for some *deus ex machina* as an antidote to feeling helpless—some sign of immortality, some deity born out of stars to realign the planet. But the starman's address rejects such simple answers: from his chariot of stars he refuses to partake in earthly affairs and warns us not to accelerate our own demise. The starman insists that it is *us*, the people, the collective mass of us, the mess of us, the song of us, that must account for its own fate. And so the people, *us*, are left back where they started, with nothing but their small selves, tumbling through the Holocene.

Yes, spirit is shaped by me, by us, by our coalition: the coalition of our sorrows and desires. This is what it means to be un-alone in all that we do, constantly moving and merging among ourselves, relinquishing our loves and lovers constantly, breaking our hearts constantly.

And then, with the starman off in some intergalactic vacuum, what do we do with ourselves, left to face each other so unguarded? We are always in pursuit of one another, yet we are always trying to run away from one another, proving that what we forego always comes circling back to us, and the inverse.

Our starman pseudohero (who is really a projection of ourselves) leaves a final message as a guide to this predicament: he singles out "children" and tells them, in an exercise of freedom, to dance. It is true that children inaugurate each era, carrying the spirit forth in their boundless receptivity, their proximity to unfiltered feeling. In the starman's address to *us*, we are the children: we must reposition ourselves within a child's configuration, within this transitional state where everything is experienced without the interruption of our worst, most volatile pollutants.

It is no coincidence that in interviews Bowie shared the influence on his songs of Nietzsche. To Nietzsche the child symbolized our greatest potential, and he once wrote, "The child is innocence and forgetting, a new beginning, a game, a self-rolling wheel, a first movement, a sacred Yes."[12] But I fear becoming another rambling interpreter of Nietzsche, so instead consider how, during the time of Müntzer's revelatory thinking in the Middle Ages, also uncoincidentally, children were depicted in art as little adults; see, for example, the late medieval painting *Ognissanti Madonna*, in which an infant Christ has the proportions of a grown man. This might imply on one hand that children were viewed as miniature adults, but on the other hand, and more importantly, this implies that in every adult is a child on the threshold, reaching out to feel everything as if constantly feeling for the first time.

So I regress into an age when we all were children, I come undone, wandering this atlas of inherited memories. As the fires turn high-rises into furnace dust, I don't long for immortality; I just want to feel someone's breath on my neck. I am scared of surrendering myself to the next moment, but I don't resist its tender envelopment. I want to feel my body fluttering through time like a sheet let loose in the wind.

And we will find each other here, wandering, curious, with a spirit that has been freed from its privatized fears, and I wonder then how we might respond to one another, what we might form together.

Would you hold me close? Would you clasp your hands around my throat?

Tiktaalik

Life on land is so feeble
an occurrence; my grandmother's
varicose limbs dip into the pondwater
dangling from this languid bridge where he,
my grandfather, sews sky to sea
with the line of his fishing pole.

Infinitely impressed by the false dignity of her own species
she begins to tell me about anatomy
etching vivisections with her words. I feel
breath through my lungs and the morphology of
wristbones revolving as I splash water into a glittering arch.
Beside me another fisherman is leafing through

the guts of his latest victory.
His fingers are hooks that fan out like flippers
and my eyes blend with the endless current.
Some years ago, my grandmother explains,
they found the fossil that tethered us to the very waters we dump our piss into,
its joints linking together the dorsal fin and human spine,

our ancestors from the brine.
My arms are sly charlatans, I feel deceived
and the pond's surface hurts my eyes—
that my guilelessness could have been so crushed, my body such a con artist
selling me death for a bargain.
If evolution brought us out of the ocean, she asks,

then where do we go from here?
The scorched afternoon sets ablaze the fish flung
from the pond's sanctum by my grandfather's baited line, it flails
allegro, a grand jeté, landing on the wooden planks of the bridge
from which my grandmother unhooks its jaw and holds it for a moment
before throwing it back, and finally the water
falls silent.

I am stung by a paper wasp on the eve of blooming

         What is this skin that gives
so willingly, so artlessly, that opens so heartily
to the welcoming of the vespid point
at which I find myself flung into the swelter
of the unforgiving afternoon, a heat stroking
my hair, a fever with wings. Paper wasp,
gentle agony, my wakening warden, the quick kiss
of a stinger that seals this puncture, the globule of blood
birthed from the entry wound: one moment I am collecting
wildflowers, the next I weep to my mother who this time
cannot fix me, so I lie supine over dandelions
whose seeds are blowing away and dream of
chasing after them—to spite my mother
and this tinctured summer—or just to see
how they too are strange and spiteful. Fetter the urge
to kiss strangers, to kick the earth, run off,
to rediscover the precarity of an open field and sink into it and bloom
like it hurts; I watch the dandelion seeds become placid cataclysms consumed
mid-ascent by their boundless ambition.
         Say paper wasp
to put a name to what aches as the sunrise aches to burn everything
on the horizon, crimson orange ochre
overflowing from the seam in the sky, in my skin, my slacks,
in my loins rising, my kneecaps hardening so one day
I may be able to build a home or break one, soon
I shall gather my longings and burn them, swallow my pride,
a simple act of unclinging, of unraveling old clothes,
opening my body to the possibility of stinging,
the tender threat of blooming

How the Price System is Like a Body: Snapshots

"In America, the big get bigger and the small go out."
—Sonny Perdue, former U.S. Secretary of Agriculture[13]

Until the 5th of December we have to spread our crumbs
keep our tummies calm with chamomile and warm blankets.

In warm blankets my mother holds me like I'm her last savings account.
We watch forest fires from the window both thinking, not speaking

of how fires can get you rescued.
Sister washing dishes, our father stuck in bed, blanketless,

hoping that we couldn't see him.
We're all trying to hide these days, waiting patiently to be saved.

On TV we watch how other people exist:
pink-ruffled girls cooking cupcakes, trays serving subservient suburban patriarchies

farmers dying in their fields, politicians eating with their hands.
Our neighbor pointed us to a McDonald's down the road,

then complained about the obesity rate.
My mother reads her cookbook like the Bible.

Dad, when not collapsed in bed, cooks frantically at a roadside joint,
for means of staying stable, or as close as possible.

He cashes desperation on mortgage debts, then gasoline,
then me, for a future university, and the rest—hardly fitting

in a closed door slit—goes to groceries.
On the 5th of December, the stamps arrive finally,

looking fed up and finicky like a kid at daycare
who must share the toy he took for himself.

My mother turns the teakettle on, and we try to guess
how long they'll persevere

until the New Year, if it ever comes.

Liner Notes for a Factory Fire[14]

It is difficult to imagine inhabiting a body other than this body which has held you captive for 13 years. Your eyes lately have been landing on the brazen danger zones of other people's bodies: an earlobe curving into the jaw, a twisting bicep, the back of some boy's shin as he walks towards an exit. And outside, the early snow which is coagulating in the road closes in around him like a ravenous ghost.

Maybe you have not been taught to conceptualize the electric ether of another living body whose every action responds to what moves between us, stunning us into life, or maybe there is just something static in all of it, in the heat and exasperation, your legs shaking, the crashing waves of his breath as he flows closer to you, drawing you in. Maybe you can't call a first kiss a kiss at all, but an excavation, a rummaging for answers on a twin-sized bed (hoping he can't tell your legs are shaking in the dark).

The afterglow of his mouth is still inside of you when you see the factory fire blazing across the TV screen—117 confirmed dead—narrow exits—American outsourcing. There are people at the scene clutching their throats as they watch their loved ones' bodies sublimate into ashen storm clouds, but not many others seem to care. At first you feel yourself pulled taut between these parallel occurrences, at one pole sparks of love and salvation pressed against your lips, and at the other, fragility, destruction, your body a disposable appliance—you are a vacancy to be either filled with sensitivity or burned to the ground, your body is an unfixed form nonetheless finite and susceptible.

And then you see your life multiply before you, split into these divergent bodies, occurring in sequence, almost at once, like a montage of wilting lilies: you are kissing a stranger on a twin-sized bed; you are a factory worker in Bangladesh rushing to cram through the exit; you are the boy who smells like hemlock and immortality, who is spilling past the horizon of your bodies—and in between these lives the "you" of yourself loosens into an echo, bouncing off the stratosphere.

You want to tell someone that it's not fair, but who would argue otherwise. You want to hold space and time on trial, insisting they have deceived us all into believing we are going somewhere. You want to un-learn empty words like me and *eternity*, throw yourself into the ocean just so you can feel yourself succumb to something larger than yourself.

But the embers are already fading into charcoaled rubble just as production has moved its exploitation elsewhere under the false prom-ise of passable working conditions, and the boy who you wanted most has just informed you that he is transferring schools to another state, and you watch him leave, become enveloped in the early snowfall—his outline is hardly visible now—as you let your body shiver uncontrollably in the cold.

Valences (A Contrapuntal)

My love, my life blood,

        tiredness never puts me to sleep—

I feel coursing through me

        the steady thrums of

the heartbeat of my mother,

        the doctrines of Thomas Müntzer battering

budding in my throat

        like the opening of a long-awaited letter

History and affinity

        forever linger on the remnants of the night—

clutch me in their dark tangle—

        cosmology meets its consequences

in the flora of strangers whirring by,

        in our weekly expenses

or in the arms of an expended mother,

where our bodies are yes breached by each other,

every elbow shifting through a crowd

        every transaction toiled for, every

reaching towards the emptiness,

        longing towards some synthesis

every person is nothing more than a bundle
        of valences, pulsating across history,
of these endless convergences
            a coming together of forces
    beyond physics
                that bind us together:
keeping me awake through the night:
                I'm on my knees,
    I'm on my knees
        gasping for breath.
        My love, my life blood,
        give me your resilience.

Exegesis of My Lover

I conjure a place
where no roads lead
and my head is bathed in
the wingless flight
of breathing and being
breathed on where
my love-drive and death-drive
have learned the passions
of unpacking their
tangled aims and
the hands of a lonely
man whose longing is like mine
light a dozen candles along
my back
as he tells me love
feels like this like not
cognizing but just perceiving
because like all things
that are filtered through consciousness
it's distorted by the process and
we will live in a cabin
in Switzerland where
my limbs are our limbs reaching
into the placid lake surface
that feels like his tongue
in my cheek that tastes like
a brazen heart or
the possibility of homoerotic love
without that tense ever-presence
of the presentiment that it will
inevitably flatline and
we will make Swiss fondue and
fuck under the Alpen
moon with our breaths winding
towards the heavens where
everything's resonant and

he will offer me this
tea and long-suffered retreat
until one day he will move
his hand away, lower his eyes,
and say we cannot be to each other
what we need,
       and I will wonder how many men
will have to unlearn one another
before the ice caps melt into oceans.

Nocturne for Running

We should have been orphans
or born out of oysters
spitting salt from our mouths before kissing our mothers
goodbye. I have not come to terms with
what a human body is
except maybe a plea for love
or for forgiveness.
On the East River I am waiting for an explosion
in the night, a sign of God or of godless survival,
the destination of every kid who has attempted flight.
People come here to redeem a past version of the self
that they can't flee: I see you
in every train car that comes and goes
over the water, like the episodic retrieval of memory,
like a passing thought of dying.

I do it because of cinema, desperation, and trips to the ocean
where we veered far enough from home
to feel limitless, because
we are born into a web that has already been spun
and all we can do is keep spinning.
I do it because I remember your face
that read: "just because," because of loneliness,
because of knowing this, watching store clerks grow old,
ditching the car and our families
in an urgent attempt to feel inviolable.
When I was 16 I wrote a poem that goes:
sometimes you don't even look up and you find yourself
running down the road. I have not
even looked up and I see you now, D–, and me, running
towards that obscure place at the edge of adolescence,
dirt in your shoes, not certain whether
it's even real (and I'm still not):
I do it for you.

Hymn for Haggard Seraphim

I spent the day reading letters that were never sent (found in furnaces, crumpled on the streets), allowing language to pulse through me like standing under a waterfall full of endless soliloquies, confessions galore. Why don't we say the things we want to say? Why do we wash them through with shampoo and bleach, letting our stampeding meanings spill out the back of our heads, never to be spoken? So I am writing to you now, and I promise not to pour my words into the flames.

On the dock of an empty and cold Coney Island, I am in the September of my lamentation, liminal, transitional. Having grown up, I am mostly tired and always longing for something which I had not understood when I had it. Perhaps the appropriate metaphor for this is a clock made of goodbye kisses. The sensation of survival fermented in the lips parting from yours, splitting into threads and then breaking off: this, over and over again until you've forgotten how glorious they once tasted, is growing up.

I am constructing an imitation of the waves below me. They come at sporadic intervals, like my memories, like the unpatterned splatter of semen on car seat polyester, a selective natality.

I choose words because words preserve instances and present instances as cohesive wholes. Forging these words is the same act as forging a violin, in which every note is immanent and can be experienced again and again, brought to life every time it is strummed, eternally, insofar as eternity is a measure of human existence. Hear these words resonate with the slide of a bow: summer becoming autumn becoming winter becoming the waves grasping for my feet, the wind of transitional states, a car crash, poverty, catastrophe, redemption—

The holy asteroid is suspended above me, twinkling and pitiless. No doubt it will soon enter Earth's atmosphere and melt the flesh off our bones. I upturn the contents of my stomach onto the dock and read them like a haruspex. I see youth and forgetting, longing and forgiveness. I see your body disappearing into a cocoon of fog. I see tectonic plates overlapping, crashing, coming together with such force that they burst into oblivion: an allegory for love?

And then I see forms materializing out of the ocean—and this isn't an augury—luminous forms, winged seraphim, who seem at once capable of commanding every aspect of matter and antimatter. I feel like I am looking at God, or whatever orgasms are made of. Yet the seraphim are distinctly human, perhaps overstatedly human—bags under their eyes, the pallor of anxiety, even their noble wings are wilted under the great pressure of human thrownness. They begin to move towards the shore, and I become shrouded in rippling shadow, met by the force of these bodies whose names are themselves signifiers for what our species amounts to: I see Joachim of Flora, Jean de Roquetaillade, and Thomas Müntzer, their faces solemn and illuminated; I see Marx and my mother, somehow known to each other; I see Saint Hildegard and Edith Maxwell, and then Bowie.

Oh Bowie, my Lady Stardust, my seraph of sound and vision, I remember when they put up a memorial cutout of you on Coney Island in front of the Wonder Wheel, some strange analogy for time. I remember how we played you on long drives to nowhere, and that, perhaps, was the more fitting analogy.

Bowie, D—, you whose features seem to fuse into a single image, you for whom I wait with a tinge of relief for the end of the world, a necessary climax of loss. It is you, the pulsating absence of you, who make every instant collapse into the next, churning me in its riptide.

Time elapses persistently, which is to say that things change so slightly that they escape awareness, like spiders spinning webs where you'd never suspect. Light switches go on and off repeatedly, even when you aren't looking. Storm clouds purge themselves and then run away. I don't know what I want more: to fix the things that I didn't know could be fixed, or to feel them passing through me like the light of stars through a telescope.

The seraphim warn me that I can't afford to dwell on these things, but that is all I'm capable of in this pounding heat, all I know is the way time is felt in relation to other people. It is true, I don't believe in millionaires or inheritance, but I am not strictly a collectivist; individual freedom does not equal accumulation of wealth. It is part of something less procedural, more expansive, that we are left to ourselves to make sense of, and when the asteroid meets our fields there will be nothing left but ash and our absence, and if this is what we are doomed to become, then only our partiality to one another is preventing us from jumping off a rooftop or running into traffic or giving ourselves into the waters of unclean beaches, but we are figuring things out together—how to breathe underwater, how to miss warning signs, what we were and will become and why—you and I are existing at the same instant which is already becoming the next, and D—, I am watching the sky at the same time as you, and I share the same uncertainties, uncertainties about what we have ruined and lost, about our mothers and our jobs, about our deaths, about each other, but no one is safe in the end, no matter how overprotective or negligent our parents are, so let us speak with candor and not hold anything else in, just hold this to your chest and imagine that you are standing under a waterfall made of all the words we should have said long ago.

Sonnet for an Apocalypse

How innocuous seems the comet from afar
like a halo of threaded gold unspooling
towards us, upon which to make a wish
before its imminent collision with our planet.
It casts a dark incandescence over the jagged streets,
the people pooling up in bars, slipping wishes into
each other's drinks. It tumbles closer, closer,
smoldering through, unzipping the night.
And in this passing light you are unzipping,
undoing all the buttons, our fingers are fumbling
waistbands and what we've learned of touch.
Cataclysms unfurl in our limbs in motion
and the comet reflects off your eyes, instantaneously
our heartbeats become an explosion.

FOOTNOTES

"Hymn for the Harvest"

[1] Michel de Montaigne, "That to Philosophise Is to Learn to Die," in *Essays of Montaigne*, Vol. 1 (New York: Edwin C. Hill, 1910), pp. 179-213).

[2] David Bowie, "Five Years," track 1 on *The Rise and Fall of Ziggy Stardust and the Spiders from Mars*, RCA, 1972.

[3] Ibid.

[4] Hildegard Von Bingen, "Vision 7 - The Devil," trans. Columba Hart and Jane Bishop, in *Hildegard of Bingen: Scivias* (1990: Paulist Press), https://www.pbs.org/wgbh/pages/frontline/shows/apocalypse/primary/scivias.html

[5] John of Rupescissa, *Vade mecum in tribulatione*, trans. Leah DeVun, in *Alchemy, Prophecy, and the End of Time: John of Rupescissa in the Late Middle Ages* ((New York, Columbia University Press: 2009), p. 35).

[6] Ibid.

[7] Thomas Müntzer, "The Prague Manifesto," trans. Peter Matheson, in *The Collected Works of Thomas Müntzer* (1988: Edinburgh), https://www.andydrummond.net/muentzer/PDFs/praguemanifesto.pdf

"Willing & Able"

[8] In 1935, in rural Virginia, Edith Maxwell was found guilty of murdering her father with a high-heeled shoe after he threatened to beat her for coming home late. This quote, and an interview with Maxwell after her imprisonment, was found in a newspaper clipping from 1935 (Marshall, Marguerite Mooere. "Edith Maxwell Says There's Nothing in Past to Regret." *New York Journal*, November 26, 1935).

"The Ecstasy of Saint Hildegard"

[9] All italicized text comes from Hildegard von Bingen's *Scivias*.

"Hymn for the Holocene"

[10] Raymond Williams, "Structures of Feeling," in *Marxism and Literature* (Oxford: Oxford University Press, 1977), pp. 128-217).

[11] David Bowie, "Starman," track 4 on *The Rise and Fall of Ziggy Stardust and the Spiders from Mars*, RCA, 1972.

[12] David Bowie, interview by Guillaume Durand, France 2, 2002; Friedrich Nietzsche, *Thus Spoke Zarathustra: a Book for All and None*, trans. Walter Kaufmann (New York: Modern Library, 1995).

"How the Price System is Like a Body: Snapshots"

[13] Perdue said this on a visit to Wisconsin Dairy Farms in 2019 in an address to local farmers. He also led the USDA in enacting a rule that removed over 700,000 people from Supplemental Nutrition Assistance Program (SNAP) benefits. "Food-stamp changes are about getting people back to work not kicking them out, says USDA chief," CNBC (CNBC, December 4, 2019).

"Liner Notes for a Factory Fire"

[14] In 2012, a fire broke out in a garment factory in Dhaka, Bangladesh. Due to the overcrowded factory space and the narrowly constructed exits, 117 were killed by the fire, with additionally over 200 people injured. The factory served several Western companies, including Walmart and Carrefour.

CREATOR'S BIO

René Bennett writes at the meeting point of desire and catastrophe. His work has been published in *Hobart Pulp*, *Expat Press*, *Fourteen Hills Magazine*, *Ligeia Magazine*, *SCAB Magazine*, and others, and has been featured in the exhibition Yours, (SVA Galleries, 2024).

www.ingramcontent.com/pod-product-compliance
Lightning Source LLC
Chambersburg PA
CBHW031258120626
46545CB00007B/2878